J577.636
RID

# The Secret Pool

Kimberly Ridley

Illustrated by Rebekah Raye

TILBURY HOUSE, PUBLISHERS ⬛ GARDINER, MAINE

# A shimmer. A twinkling.
Do you have any inkling of what I am?

Even if you are lucky enough to find me shining on the forest floor on an early spring day, you might mistake me for a puddle—which I most certainly am not!

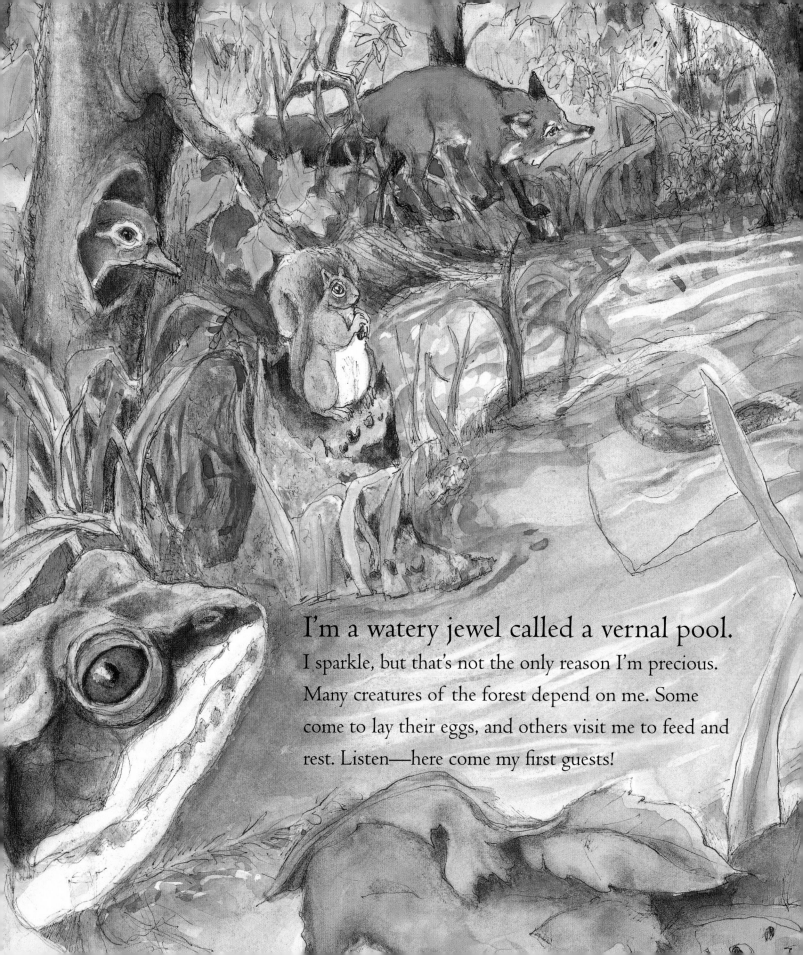

I'm a watery jewel called a vernal pool.
I sparkle, but that's not the only reason I'm precious.
Many creatures of the forest depend on me. Some
come to lay their eggs, and others visit me to feed and
rest. Listen—here come my first guests!

## What's a Vernal Pool?

*Vernal* means "occurring in spring," which is when you can find vernal pools. These temporary pools can be as small as a puddle or as big as a pond. They form every year when low places in the land fill up with rain, or in colder climates, with melted snow.

Vernal pools are found around the world and are identified by the creatures that breed in them. In the northeastern United States and eastern Canada, these include wood frogs, spotted salamanders, and fairy shrimp. Vernal pools usually dry up in late summer, which means fish and other predators that need water year round can't live in them. That's a good thing, because fish would eat the creatures that breed in vernal pools, along with their eggs!

## Spring's First Singers

A great way to find a vernal pool is to listen for wood frogs in very early spring. They sound like quacking ducks!

Wood frogs survive the winter in an amazing way. They crawl under the leaves and freeze into "frogsicles." Ice crystals form inside their bodies, but wood frogs make a special, sugary chemical called glycol that keeps them from freezing solid. Their hearts stop beating and they stop breathing all winter long, but they wake up again when their bodies thaw out in the spring rains and warmer air temperatures. Soon, they hop back to vernal pools to mate and lay their eggs—often in the same pool where they were hatched. After breeding, wood frogs return to land, where they spend the summer eating spiders, beetles, earthworms, and other invertebrates.

"Cruck, crrruuuck, CRRRRUUUCK!!!

My first spring visitors sound like ducks, but guess again.
Come closer and all you see are old brown leaves. Wait. One of
the leaves is moving. Aha, it's a wood frog! The males float on my
surface and call loudly, looking for mates. Their song is not sweet,
but it breaks the winter's silence.

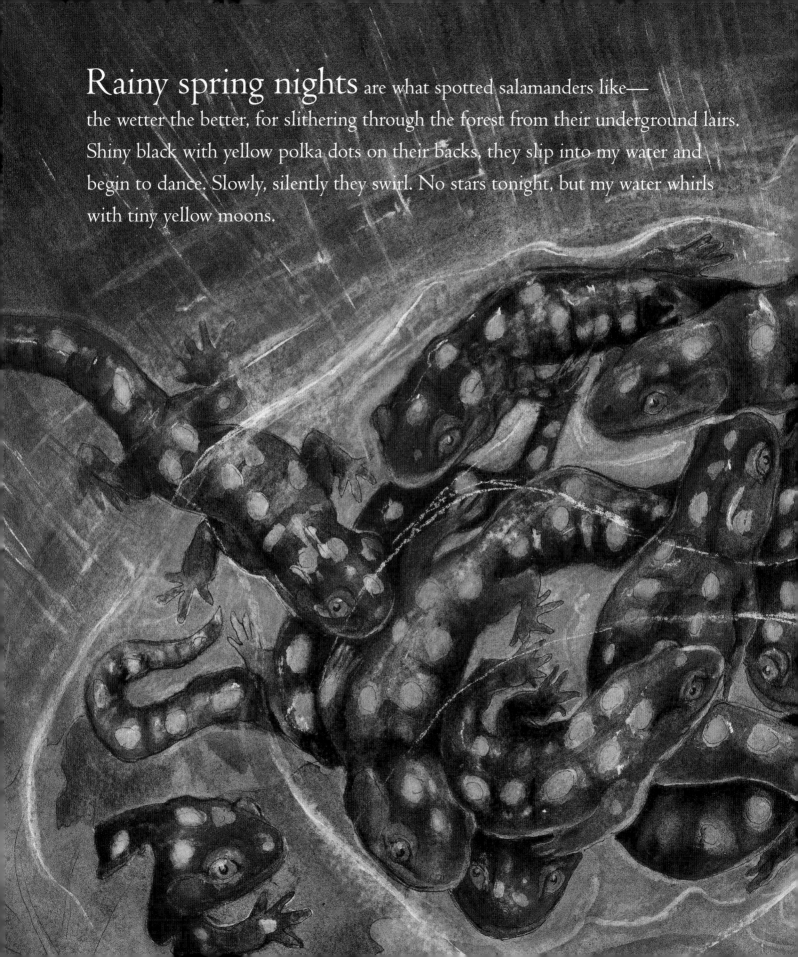

Rainy spring nights are what spotted salamanders like—
the wetter the better, for slithering through the forest from their underground lairs.
Shiny black with yellow polka dots on their backs, they slip into my water and
begin to dance. Slowly, silently they swirl. No stars tonight, but my water whirls
with tiny yellow moons.

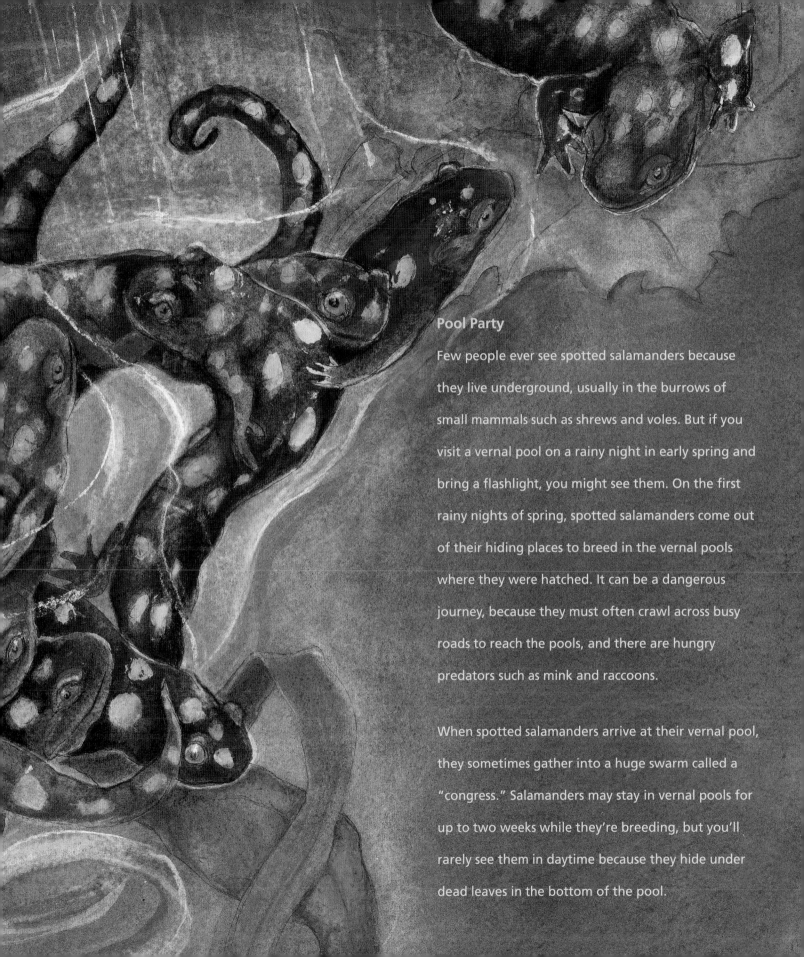

## Pool Party

Few people ever see spotted salamanders because they live underground, usually in the burrows of small mammals such as shrews and voles. But if you visit a vernal pool on a rainy night in early spring and bring a flashlight, you might see them. On the first rainy nights of spring, spotted salamanders come out of their hiding places to breed in the vernal pools where they were hatched. It can be a dangerous journey, because they must often crawl across busy roads to reach the pools, and there are hungry predators such as mink and raccoons.

When spotted salamanders arrive at their vernal pool, they sometimes gather into a huge swarm called a "congress." Salamanders may stay in vernal pools for up to two weeks while they're breeding, but you'll rarely see them in daytime because they hide under dead leaves in the bottom of the pool.

## Shrimpy Shrimp

You might think shrimp just live in the ocean, but tiny, mysterious fairy shrimp can only live in vernal pools and other temporary wetlands formed from rain or melted snow. You will be very lucky if you see fairy shrimp, because they don't live in all vernal pools, they only live about six weeks, and they are very small. The biggest fairy shrimp are only about one to one-and-one-half inches long.

Fairy shrimp usually hatch in very early spring and sometimes again later in the summer. They tend to gather in sunny patches in vernal pools. Fairy shrimp eat microscopic animals called zooplankton, which can affect the color of their bodies.

Fairy shrimp lay their tiny eggs on the bottom of vernal pools. These eggs must dry out completely and freeze in order to hatch the following spring. Some fairy shrimp eggs can last fifteen years before hatching!

Other creatures have laid their eggs in me, like dark little dots almost too small to see. But when they hatch, ka-boom! I am filled with jazzy orange fairy shrimp. Slim and frilly, they swim willy-nilly upside down, tickling me with their feathery feet.

Gone are the salamanders,
along with the frogs. They've returned to dry land
and their mossy bogs. But what have they left behind?
Hundreds of slippery, slimy surprise packages. Now
I'm all lumpy and bumpy with clumps of their eggs.

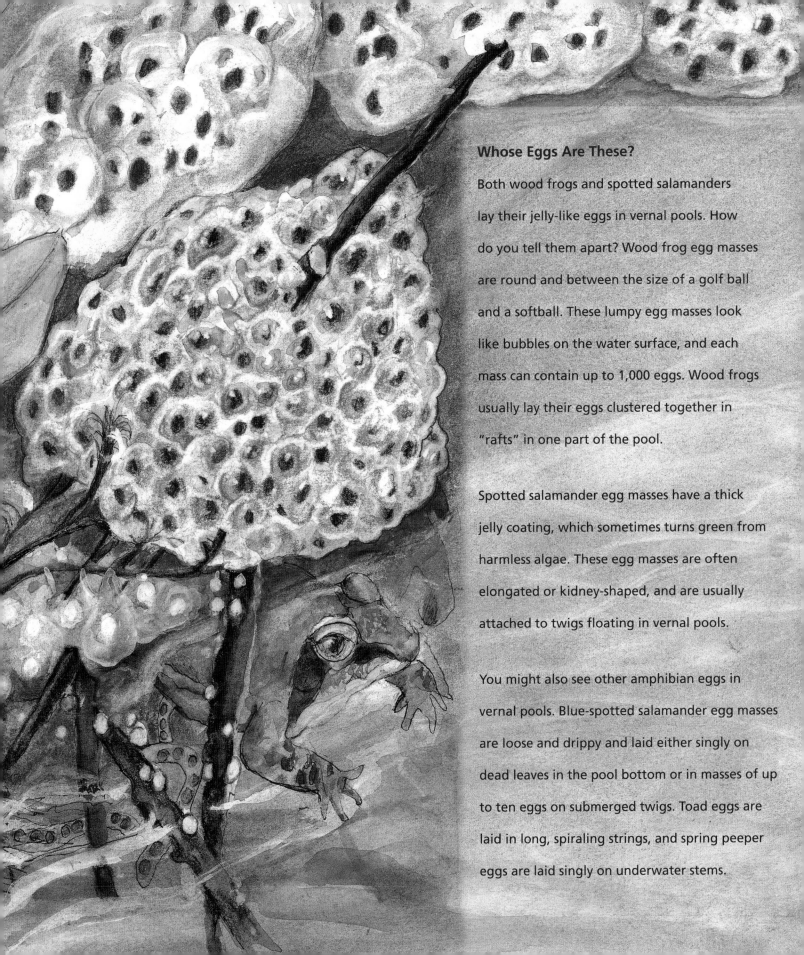

## Whose Eggs Are These?

Both wood frogs and spotted salamanders lay their jelly-like eggs in vernal pools. How do you tell them apart? Wood frog egg masses are round and between the size of a golf ball and a softball. These lumpy egg masses look like bubbles on the water surface, and each mass can contain up to 1,000 eggs. Wood frogs usually lay their eggs clustered together in "rafts" in one part of the pool.

Spotted salamander egg masses have a thick jelly coating, which sometimes turns green from harmless algae. These egg masses are often elongated or kidney-shaped, and are usually attached to twigs floating in vernal pools.

You might also see other amphibian eggs in vernal pools. Blue-spotted salamander egg masses are loose and drippy and laid either singly on dead leaves in the pool bottom or in masses of up to ten eggs on submerged twigs. Toad eggs are laid in long, spiraling strings, and spring peeper eggs are laid singly on underwater stems.

### Wood Frog Tadpoles

Wood frog eggs are the first amphibian eggs to hatch in vernal pools. The tiny tadpoles are usually herbivorous, which means they feed on plants. If they can't find enough food, however, they'll eat each other, as well as the eggs of other amphibians!

Jiggling and wriggling. Something big is happening. Wood frog tadpoles burst from their bubbly eggs. They squiggle free and eat algae and other tasty treats that grow on my leafy floor.

Baby salamanders stalk their prey at night. Just like their parents, they shun the light. Tiny, but ferocious, they will eat any little thing that moves—including each other. Look out!

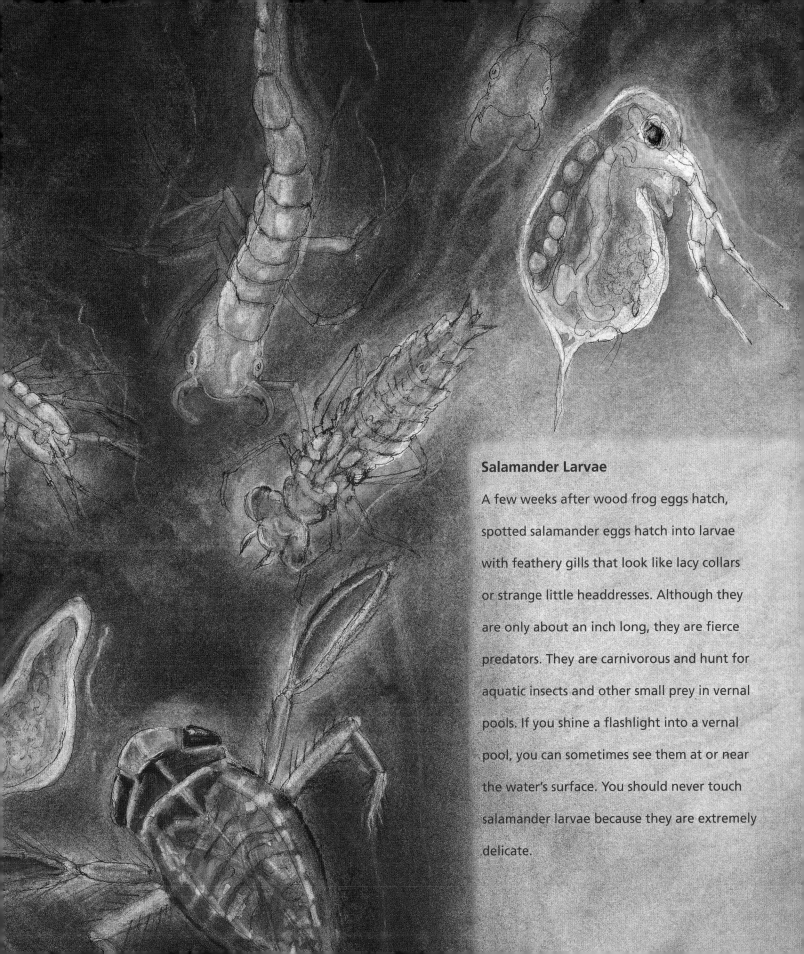

### Salamander Larvae

A few weeks after wood frog eggs hatch, spotted salamander eggs hatch into larvae with feathery gills that look like lacy collars or strange little headdresses. Although they are only about an inch long, they are fierce predators. They are carnivorous and hunt for aquatic insects and other small prey in vernal pools. If you shine a flashlight into a vernal pool, you can sometimes see them at or near the water's surface. You should never touch salamander larvae because they are extremely delicate.

Ker-plop. KER-PLUNK! A hungry bullfrog is on the hunt.
Tadpoles scatter in every direction—except the ones he catches for lunch.

## Pool Hopping

Scientists have tracked bullfrogs and turtles traveling from pool to pool to feast on tadpoles and eggs. Ribbon snakes and other snakes also hang out around vernal pools for easy meals.

By summer, my waters wiggle with lots of creatures sprouting all kinds of dandy new features. They must grow legs and lungs before it's too late. Even then, the chances they'll make it aren't always so great. Hurry up!

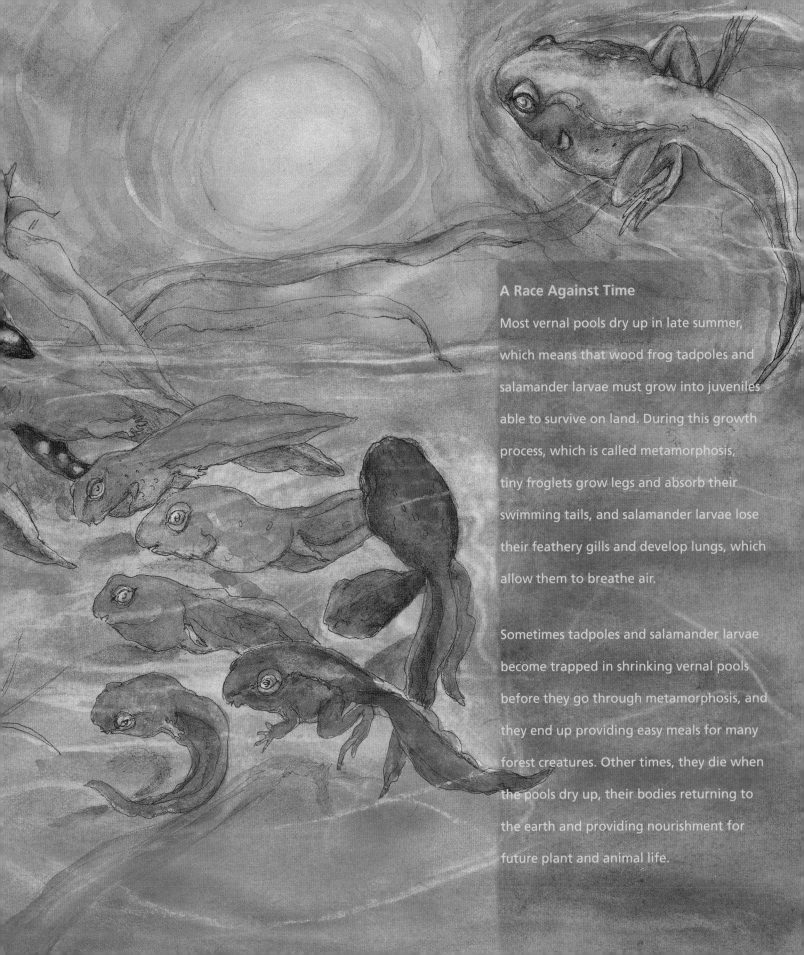

## A Race Against Time

Most vernal pools dry up in late summer, which means that wood frog tadpoles and salamander larvae must grow into juveniles able to survive on land. During this growth process, which is called metamorphosis, tiny froglets grow legs and absorb their swimming tails, and salamander larvae lose their feathery gills and develop lungs, which allow them to breathe air.

Sometimes tadpoles and salamander larvae become trapped in shrinking vernal pools before they go through metamorphosis, and they end up providing easy meals for many forest creatures. Other times, they die when the pools dry up, their bodies returning to the earth and providing nourishment for future plant and animal life.

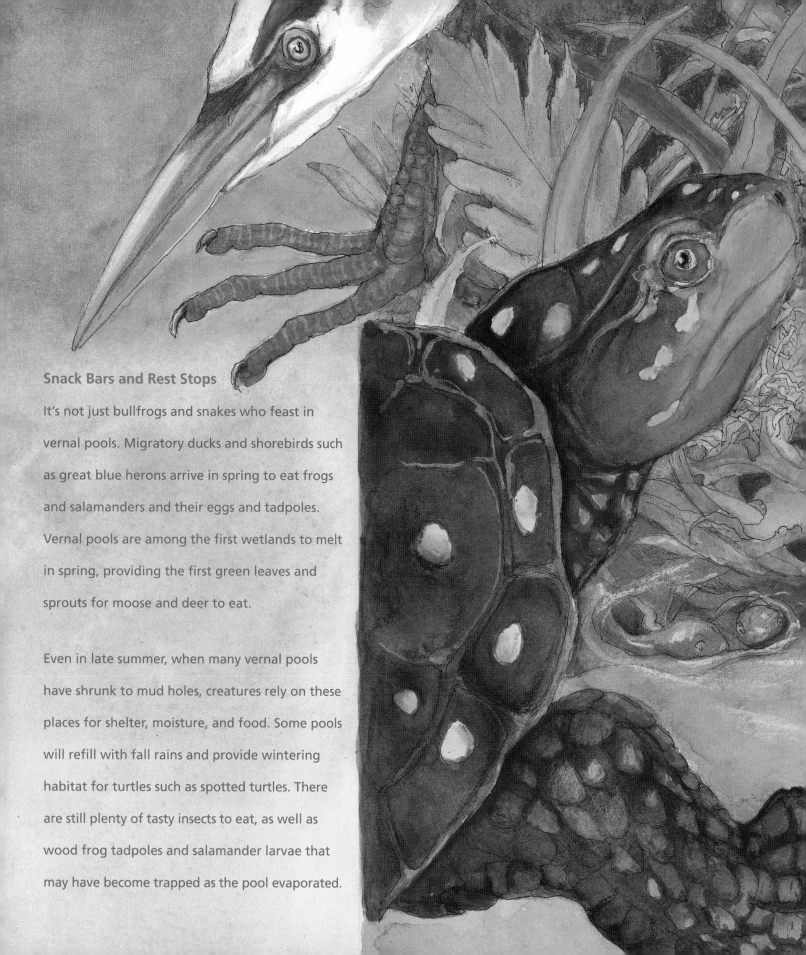

## Snack Bars and Rest Stops

It's not just bullfrogs and snakes who feast in
vernal pools. Migratory ducks and shorebirds such
as great blue herons arrive in spring to eat frogs
and salamanders and their eggs and tadpoles.
Vernal pools are among the first wetlands to melt
in spring, providing the first green leaves and
sprouts for moose and deer to eat.

Even in late summer, when many vernal pools
have shrunk to mud holes, creatures rely on these
places for shelter, moisture, and food. Some pools
will refill with fall rains and provide wintering
habitat for turtles such as spotted turtles. There
are still plenty of tasty insects to eat, as well as
wood frog tadpoles and salamander larvae that
may have become trapped as the pool evaporated.

My work this year is nearly done, and I'm disappearing with the summer sun. I'm shrinking and sinking into the earth. But I still feed hungry creatures lurking around.

A whisper of wet is all that I am, a small muddy patch on the frosty land. Trees drop their leaves and cover me up. You might think I've disappeared, but don't worry. I'm just getting ready for next year.

**Migration Isn't Just for the Birds**

Although they don't travel as far as the birds,
wood frogs and spotted salamanders migrate, too.
In spring, adult amphibians migrate to their vernal
pools to breed, and then they migrate to other
habitats to feed and rest for the summer.

Later on, young wood frogs and salamanders migrate
from the vernal pools where they were hatched to
find habitat on land for the rest of summer, fall, and
winter. Some young wood frogs travel more than half
a mile—that's a lot of hopping!

I've shown you my secrets, and now I must go.

It's time to make more life from **leaves**, **rain**, and **snow**.

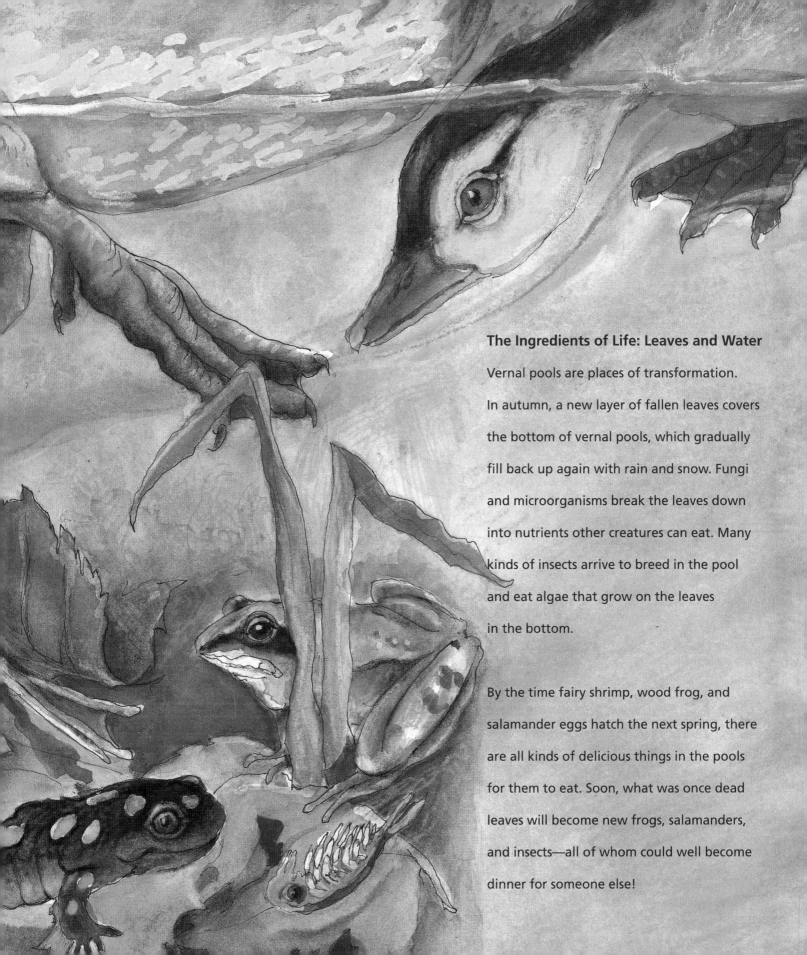

## The Ingredients of Life: Leaves and Water

Vernal pools are places of transformation. In autumn, a new layer of fallen leaves covers the bottom of vernal pools, which gradually fill back up again with rain and snow. Fungi and microorganisms break the leaves down into nutrients other creatures can eat. Many kinds of insects arrive to breed in the pool and eat algae that grow on the leaves in the bottom.

By the time fairy shrimp, wood frog, and salamander eggs hatch the next spring, there are all kinds of delicious things in the pools for them to eat. Soon, what was once dead leaves will become new frogs, salamanders, and insects—all of whom could well become dinner for someone else!

## Glossary

**algae**
tiny plants that have no true leaves, stems, or roots (singular, alga)

**amphibian**
a group of cold-blooded, smooth-skinned animals such as frogs, salamanders, toads, and newts that spend part of their lives in water and part on land

**aquatic**
living or growing in or near water

**carnivore**
a meat-eater

**fungi**
mold, mushrooms, and other organisms that feed on decaying matter (singular, fungus)

**habitat**
the place where an animal, plant, or other organism naturally lives

**hibernation**
a period of inactivity during the winter

**invertebrate**
an animal that doesn't have a backbone, such as an insect or worm

**juvenile**
a young animal or plant

**larva**
the newly hatched form of an amphibian or invertebrate, such as a tadpole or a caterpillar (plural, larvae)

**metamorphosis**
a process through which some organisms grow into adults

**microorganism**
a living being that is too small to see with the naked eye

**organism**
a living thing

**vertebrate**
an animal with a backbone

**wetlands**
places that are saturated with water, such as swamps and marshes

**zooplankton**
microscopic animals that live in water

TILBURY HOUSE, PUBLISHERS
103 Brunswick Avenue
Gardiner, Maine 04345
800–582–1899 • www.tilburyhouse.com

First hardcover edition: October 1, 2013 • 10 9 8 7 6 5 4 3 2 1

To Thomas, and in loving memory of my father, Russell J. Ridley. —KR
For my father, Ray E. Bradley. May he always be as close as a whisper. —RR

Thanks to Dr. Aram Calhoun, professor of Wetlands Ecology, University of Maine, and to her
colleague, Dawn Morgan, for reviewing the text and for sharing their vast knowledge of vernal pools.
Heartfelt gratitude to my writers' group: Ellen Booraem, Ann Logan, Becky McCall, Gail Page, and
Susa Wuorinen, for their brilliance and encouragement. Thanks also to my young readers, Eliza, Quin,
Finnegan, and Corin, whose questions and comments were a great help. I am grateful beyond words to
my dear friend Rebekah Raye for bringing the pool and its creatures magnificently to life with her art,
and to Jennifer Bunting and Audrey Maynard for their care and support. Finally, this book wouldn't have
happened without Tom Curry, whose love, belief, and willingness to traipse around with me on rainy
spring nights to look for salamanders have made all the difference. —KR

Library of Congress Cataloging-in-Publication Data
Ridley, Kimberly.
  The secret pool / Kimberly Ridley ; illustrated by Rebekah Raye.
      pages cm
  Audience: 6-8.
  Audience: K to grade 3.
  ISBN 978-0-88448-339-7 (hardcover : alk. paper)
  1. Vernal pools. 2. Vernal pool ecology. 3. Pond animals.  I. Raye, Rebekah. II. Title.
  QH541.5.P63R53 2013\
  577.63'6—dc23
                                    2013006032

Designed by Geraldine Millham, Westport, Massachusetts.
Printed and bound by Pacom Korea, Inc., Dang Jung-Dong 242-2, GungPo-si, Kyunggi-do, Korea;
June 2013.